AF481033

Celeste's Magical Chakra Quest

Printed in USA

Independent Publishing
Cover design by Denisse Zapata
First Edition: May, 2024

For permissions or inquiries, please contact the Author at
spiritstarseeds@gmail.com

DEAR PARENTS,

I am delighted to share "Celeste's Magical Chakra Quest" with you and your children. This book is crafted with love and a deep sense of purpose, designed to guide young readers on a captivating journey through the chakras, uncovering the magic that lies within each of us.

As your child follows Celeste's enchanting adventures, they will explore the vibrant world of the chakras, each represented by magical realms and wise characters. From discovering inner strength and creativity to embracing love and clarity, each chapter offers a gentle lesson that encourages self-discovery and emotional growth.

This book is intended not only to entertain but to inspire. It invites children to reflect on their own feelings, strengths, and aspirations, fostering a sense of wonder and understanding. By engaging with Celeste's journey, they will learn to connect with their inner selves and recognize the beauty of their unique qualities.

I hope that Celeste's Magical Chakra Quest becomes a cherished part of your family's reading time and sparks meaningful conversations. Thank you for allowing this journey to be part of your child's adventure.

With heartfelt appreciation,

Denisse Zapata

LIGHT UP THEIR WORLD: A SPECIAL MEDITATION JOURNEY FOR YOU AND YOUR CHILD

After reading our book, we invite you to explore the "Rainbow of Light" meditation with your child. This simple and soothing practice is a wonderful way to help them connect with their inner selves, building confidence, emotional balance, and a sense of peace.

By taking just a few moments each day to practice this meditation together, you're not only nurturing your child's well-being but also creating a special bonding experience. It's a beautiful way to wind down after a busy day or to start the morning with positive energy.

Encourage your child to embrace this magical journey inside themselves, knowing that each colorful light helps them grow strong, creative, and kind. Together, you can light up their world with the power of the chakras!

Happy meditating! 🌈

RAINBOW OF LIGHT: A 7 CHAKRAS MEDITATION FOR KIDS

Hey there, little one! Today, we're going on a special adventure inside ourselves. We're going to visit the 7 chakras. These are like colorful lights inside your body that help you feel happy, strong, and peaceful. Let's sit comfortably, close our eyes, and take a big, deep breath in…and out. Now, let's begin our journey through the rainbow of light!

1. Root Chakra (Red):

Imagine a bright red light at the bottom of your spine, right where you're sitting. This red light helps you feel safe and strong, like a tree with deep roots. As you breathe in, feel the red light getting brighter and stronger, and say to yourself: "I am safe. I am strong."

Pause for a few breaths

2. Sacral Chakra (Orange):

Now, let's move up to your belly, just below your belly button. Imagine an orange light glowing there. This orange light helps you feel happy and creative, like when you're drawing or playing. Breathe in the orange light, and say to yourself: "I am happy. I am creative."

Pause for a few breaths.

3. Solar Plexus Chakra (Yellow):

Next, imagine a bright yellow light in your tummy, right where you feel butterflies when you're excited. This yellow light gives you confidence and helps you feel brave. Breathe in the yellow light, and say to yourself: "I am strong. I am confident."

Pause for a few breaths.

4. Heart Chakra (Green):

Now, let's move up to your chest, where your heart is. Imagine a warm green light glowing there. This green light is full of love and kindness. Breathe in the green light, and say to yourself: "I am loved. I am kind."

Pause for a few breaths.

5. Throat Chakra (Blue):

Next, imagine a peaceful blue light in your throat, where your voice comes from. This blue light helps you speak your truth and share your thoughts. Breathe in the blue light, and say to yourself: "I speak my truth. I am heard."

Pause for a few breaths.

6. Third Eye Chakra (Indigo):

Now, move up to the space between your eyebrows. Imagine a deep indigo light glowing there, like a star in the night sky. This indigo light helps you see clearly and use your imagination. Breathe in the indigo light, and say to yourself: "I am wise. I see clearly."

Pause for a few breaths.

7. Crown Chakra (Violet):

Finally, imagine a beautiful violet light at the top of your head, like a crown. This violet light connects you to everything around you and helps you feel peaceful. Breathe in the violet light, and say to yourself: "I am connected. I am at peace."

Pause for a few breaths.

Conclusion:

Now, take a moment to imagine all these colorful lights shining together inside you, like a beautiful rainbow. Feel how calm, happy, and strong you are. When you're ready, slowly open your eyes and bring that rainbow of light with you into the world. You did an amazing job!

MY CHAKRA REFLECTIONS

Take a moment to think about the chakras you've explored with Celeste. Use this page to share your thoughts and feelings about each chakra. What did you learn? How did each chakra make you feel? Let your creativity shine!

1. Root Chakra

How do you feel safe and strong?

2. Sacral Chakra

What makes you feel happy and creative?

3. Solar Plexus Chakra

When do you feel brave and confident?

4. Heart Chakra

How do you show love and kindness?

5. Throat Chakra

How do you express yourself?

6. Third Eye Chakra

What helps you see clearly and use your imagination?

7. Crown Chakra

When do you feel connected to the world around you?

My Chakra Journey:
Which chakra did you connect with the most? Why?

In a land where magic danced through the air and sparkling stars twinkled above, there lived an 8 year old girl named Celeste. With her golden brown hair and sparkling hazel eyes, she was always ready for a new adventure. One day, her wise grandmother Zara handed her a shimmering map. "This map will guide you on a special quest. You'll discover the magic of the seven chakras, each holding a wonderful gift for you."

THE ROOT CHAKRA

Celeste's first stop was a majestic, ancient oak tree named Oak. His roots reached deep into the earth. "Welcome, Celeste," Oak rumbled warmly. "The Root Chakra helps you feel grounded and strong. Imagine your feet growing roots into the earth, making you feel steady and secure." As Celeste placed her hands on Oak's rough bark, she felt a deep, calming connection to the earth, filling her with confidence and stability.

THE SACRAL CHAKRA

Next, Celeste met Cascade, a playful water sprite with sparkling wings who danced through a rainbow-colored lake. "Hi, Celeste!" Cascade giggled. "The Sacral Chakra is all about your emotions and creativity. Splash in the water and let your feelings guide your creativity." Celeste laughed and played, her fingers creating swirls of vibrant colors on the water's surface. She felt a rush of inspiration, discovering how joyful and freeing it was to express her emotions.

THE SOLAR PLEXUS CHAKRA

In a sunlit meadow, Celeste encountered Sol, a majestic lioness with a radiant golden mane. "The Solar Plexus Chakra is where your inner strength and confidence reside," Sol said with a proud roar. "Stand tall, believe in yourself, and let your light shine like the sun." Celeste stood confidently, feeling a warm, powerful energy inside her. She knew she could face any challenge with newfound courage.

THE HEART CHAKRA

Celeste then arrived at a serene garden filled with blooming flowers. There, she met Harmony, a gentle dove with glowing feathers. "Welcome, Celeste," Harmony cooed softly. "The Heart Chakra helps you connect with others through love and compassion. Share kindness and see how your heart expands." Celeste helped a wilted flower bloom again and comforted a small creature. She felt her heart open and fill with warmth, learning the true magic of empathy and love.

THROAT CHAKRA

Celeste continued her journey to a quiet, starry cave where Whisper, a wise owl with twinkling eyes, perched. "The Throat Chakra is about expressing your truth and listening well," Whisper hooted gently. "Speak clearly, and let your heart listen to others." Celeste practiced speaking her thoughts and listening carefully, realizing how important it was to share her feelings and understand those around her.

THE THIRD EYE CHAKRA

In a mystical forest bathed in the soft glow of fireflies,
Celeste met Luna, a shimmering unicorn with a starry coat.
"The Third Eye Chakra helps you see beyond the ordinary,"
Luna said softly. "Trust your inner vision and intuition."
Celeste closed her eyes and let her imagination guide her.
As she opened her eyes, she saw a world full of magical
possibilities, feeling her intuition grow clearer and stronger.

THE CROWN CHAKRA

Finally, Celeste climbed a magical mountain to meet Aurora, a celestial being of light. "The Crown Chakra connects you to the universe and your higher self," Aurora's voice resonated like a soft melody. "Look up at the stars and feel your connection to the cosmos." Celeste gazed at the starry sky, feeling a deep sense of unity and understanding. She felt connected to everything around her and knew her place in the grand universe.

With each chakra's gift, Celeste felt more balanced and joyful. She returned to her village with a heart full of wisdom and excitement. She shared her adventure with her friends, teaching them about the magic of the chakras and how they can help us feel strong, creative, confident, loving, clear, wise, and connected.

As the moon rose and the stars twinkled brightly, Celeste knew her journey was just beginning. With the magic of the chakras guiding her, she was ready for endless new adventures, exploring the wondrous world around her.

End of Story

ABOUT THE AUTHOR

In the mystical lands of the Andes in Lima, Perú, emerged Denisse N. Zapata, embarking on a celestial odyssey at the tender age of 26. Her soul's yearning for profound truths kindled a metamorphosis, leading her to illuminate the path for mothers and their precious offspring.

Within the tapestries of her "little alchemy tales," Denisse weaves spells of tenderness, empathy, and mindfulness, nurturing the sacred bond between parent and child. Her sacred mission unfolds as she empowers families, sowing seeds of spiritual awakening and forging connections with the ethereal realms.

Through the alchemy of workshops and personal guidance, Denisse harmonizes spiritual wisdom with holistic well-being, birthing sanctuaries where families bloom. Her unwavering commitment serves as a beacon, uniting a tribe of enlightened mothers and children, reveling in the splendor of shared voyages and the boundless magic dwelling within each soul.